LIVE IT:
OPTIMISM

ROBERT WALKER

Crabtree Publishing Company

www.crabtreebooks.com

Author: Robert Walker
Coordinating editor: Bonnie Dobkin
Publishing plan research and development:
Sean Charlebois, Reagan Miller
Crabtree Publishing Company
Editor: Reagan Miller
Proofreader: Crystal Sikkens
Editorial director: Kathy Middleton
Production coordinator: Margaret Salter
Prepress technician: Margaret Salter

Logo design: Samantha Crabtree
Project Manager: Santosh Vasudevan (Q2AMEDIA)
Art Direction: Rahul Dhiman (Q2AMEDIA)
Design: Rohit Juneja (Q2AMEDIA)
Illustrations: Q2AMEDIA
Front Cover: After being diagnosed with Parkinson's Disease,
actor Michael J. Fox is helping work toward finding a cure
and is confident he will see one in his lifetime.
Title Page: Singer Jewel performed at coffeehouses for many years,
convinced that the experience would lead her to success.

Library and Archives Canada Cataloguing in Publication

Walker, Robert, 1980-
Live it: optimism / Robert Walker.

(Crabtree character sketches)
Includes index.
ISBN 978-0-7787-4887-8 (bound).--ISBN 978-0-7787-4920-2 (pbk.)

1. Optimism--Juvenile literature. 2. Biography--Juvenile literature.
I. Title. II. Title: Optimism. III. Series: Crabtree character sketches

BJ1477.W34 2010   j179'.9   C2009-904986-4

Library of Congress Cataloging-in-Publication Data

Walker, Robert.
Live it : optimism / Robert Walker.
p. cm. -- (Crabtree character sketches)
Includes index.

ISBN 978-0-7787-4920-2 (pbk. : alk. paper) -- ISBN 978-0-7787-4887-8
(reinforced library binding : alk. paper)
1. Optimism--Juvenile literature. I. Title.

BJ1477.W35 2009
152.4--dc22
                              2009033254

Crabtree Publishing Company

www.crabtreebooks.com   1-800-387-7650

Printed in the USA/122009/BG20090930

Published in Canada
Crabtree Publishing
616 Welland Ave.
St. Catharines, ON
L2M 5V6

Published in the United States
Crabtree Publishing
PMB 59051
350 Fifth Avenue, 59th Floor
New York, New York 10118

Published in the United Kingdom
Crabtree Publishing
Maritime House
Basin Road North, Hove
BN41 1WR

Published in Australia
Crabtree Publishing
386 Mt. Alexander Rd.
Ascot Vale (Melbourne)
VIC 3032

CONTENTS

WHAT IS OPTIMISM?

OPTIMISM IS ABOUT BEING HOPEFUL AND EXPECTING THE BEST—EVEN WHEN THERE'S NO REASON TO THINK THE BEST WILL HAPPEN. IT IS IMPORTANT TO BE OPTIMISTIC WHEN YOU ARE REACHING FOR YOUR DREAMS, STRUGGLING THROUGH DIFFICULT TIMES, OR FACING WHAT SEEMS TO BE AN IMPOSSIBLE SITUATION.

THE PEOPLE IN THIS BOOK ALL SHOWED OPTIMISM IN THEIR LIVES AND INSPIRED OTHERS TO DO THE SAME. READ THEIR STORIES AND THINK ABOUT WHAT YOU WOULD DO IN SIMILAR SITUATIONS.

MICHAEL J. FOX
ACTOR, ADVOCATE FOR THE RESEARCH AND *TREATMENT* OF *PARKINSON'S DISEASE*

DANIEL "RUDY" RUETTIGER
DEFENSIVE END, NOTRE DAME FIGHTING IRISH FOOTBALL TEAM

JEWEL
WORLD-FAMOUS MUSICIAN

MARTIN LUTHER KING, JR.
CIVIL RIGHTS LEADER

ELAINE HALL
FOUNDER OF THE MIRACLE PROJECT

RED POLLARD AND SEABISCUIT
PROFESSIONAL JOCKEY AND HIS HORSE

OPTIMISM DURING ILLNESS

MICHAEL J. FOX

WHO IS HE?
ACTOR AND T.V. STAR. ALSO KNOWN FOR HIS *BACK TO THE FUTURE* MOVIES

WHY HIM?
IN 1991, MICHAEL LEARNED HE HAD PARKINSON'S DISEASE. HE CHOSE TO REMAIN HOPEFUL, WORKING TO FIND A CURE FOR THOSE LIVING WITH PARKINSON'S.

MICHAEL J. FOX KNEW HIS LIFE WOULD CHANGE WITH THE ONSET OF PARKINSON'S DISEASE. LET'S SEE HOW HE STAYED OPTIMISTIC IN THE FACE OF HIS ILLNESS.

BORN IN CANADA, MICHAEL J. FOX MADE THE MOVE TO HOLLYWOOD WHEN HE WAS STILL A TEENAGER.

HEY, I DON'T MIND IF I TOOT MY OWN HORN. TOOT! TOOT!

IT WASN'T TOO LONG BEFORE HE FOUND HIMSELF ON A HIT T.V. SHOW

MICHAEL'S **POPULARITY** CONTINUED TO GROW.

WE LOVE YOU MICHAEL!

WHO SHOULD I MAKE THIS OUT TO?

NE DAY, WHILE FILMING A MOVIE, ICHAEL NOTICED SOMETHING STRANGE.

WHAT THE-? MY PINKIE KEEPS TWITCHING, BUT I'M NOT MOVING IT.

WHEN THE TWITCHING DIDN'T STOP, HE WENT TO A DOCTOR.

I'M SORRY MICHAEL, BUT YOU HAVE PARKINSON'S DISEASE. WHEN YOU'RE READY, WE CAN TALK ABOUT TREATMENT OPTIONS.

A PERSON WITH PARKINSON'S DISEASE SLOWLY LOSES CONTROL OF HIS OR HER BODY. PARKINSON'S CAN ALSO AFFECT HOW A PERSON THINKS AND FEELS.

NIS WAS TERRIBLE NEWS FOR MICHAEL. HE AD A SERIOUS DISEASE, AND THERE WASN'T CURE. NO ONE WOULD HAVE BLAMED HIM OR LOSING HOPE.

BUT HE DIDN'T. MICHAEL DECIDED THAT IF THERE WASN'T A CURE FOR PARKINSON'S, HE WOULD DO EVERYTHING HE COULD TO HELP FIND ONE.

TODAY I'M ANNOUNCING THE MICHAEL J. FOX FOUNDATION. OUR GOAL IS TO RAISE FUNDS TO HELP THOSE LIVING WITH PARKINSON'S, AND TO FIND A CURE.

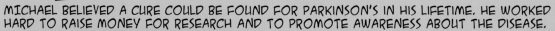

MICHAEL BELIEVED A CURE COULD BE FOUND FOR PARKINSON'S IN HIS LIFETIME. HE WORKED HARD TO RAISE MONEY FOR RESEARCH AND TO PROMOTE AWARENESS ABOUT THE DISEASE.

HE SPOKE BEFORE CONGRESS.

HE ORGANIZED FUNDRAISERS.

HE WENT ON TALK SHOWS TO DISCUSS HIS BATT WITH THE DISEASE AND ENCOURAGE PEOPLE TO JOIN THE FIGHT TO FIND A CURE.

BUT EVEN MORE IMPRESSIVE WAS THE WAY MICHAEL USED HIS ILLNESS TO BRING POSITIVE CHANGE INTO HIS LIFE.

HIGHER, DADDY!

IF I HADN'T GOTTEN SICK, I WOULD STILL BE TAKING DAYS LIKE THIS FOR GRANTED.

LEARNING HE HAD PARKINSON'S MADE MICHAEL APPRECIATE HIS WIFE AND KID EVEN MORE. HE BEGAN SPENDING EXTR TIME WITH HIS FAMILY AND FRIENDS.

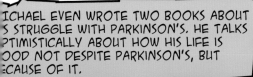

MICHAEL EVEN WROTE TWO BOOKS ABOUT HIS STRUGGLE WITH PARKINSON'S. HE TALKS OPTIMISTICALLY ABOUT HOW HIS LIFE IS GOOD NOT DESPITE PARKINSON'S, BUT BECAUSE OF IT.

MICHAEL J. FOX

Lucky MAN

ALWAYS LOOKING UP

The Adventures of an Incurable Optimist

FOR EVERYTHING THIS DISEASE HAS TAKEN, SOMETHING WITH GREATER VALUE HAS BEEN GIVEN—SOMETIMES JUST A MARKER THAT POINTS ME IN A NEW DIRECTION THAT I MIGHT NOT OTHERWISE HAVE TRAVELED.*

*ACTUAL QUOTE

IT'S AMAZING HOW MICHAEL HAS REMAINED OPTIMISTIC THROUGHOUT HIS ILLNESS. INSTEAD OF GIVING UP, HE WORKS TO FIND A CURE, SPENDS TIME WITH FAMILY AND FRIENDS, AND ENJOYS HIS LIFE. NOW, LET'S SEE WHAT YOU WOULD DO IN A SIMILAR SITUATION.

WHAT WOULD YOU DO?

YOU WANT TO TRY OUT FOR THE BASEBALL TEAM AT SCHOOL. TWO DAYS BEFORE TRYOUTS, YOU BREAK YOUR ARM. A WEEK LATER, YOU FIND OUT THAT SOME OF YOUR BEST FRIENDS MADE THE TEAM.

YOU MIGHT WANT TO FEEL SORRY FOR YOURSELF AND SIT IN YOUR ROOM FOR THE REST OF THE SEASON. BUT HOW COULD YOU TURN THIS NEGATIVE SITUATION INTO A POSITIVE EXPERIENCE?

RUDY

WHO IS HE?
DEFENSIVE END FOR THE NOTRE DAME FIGHTING IRISH FOOTBALL TEAM

WHY HIM?
RUDY'S OPTIMISM EARNED HIM A SPOT ON THE NOTRE DAME FOOTBALL TEAM

> AT 5'6" (1.7 METERS) AND 165 POUNDS (74.8 KG), RUDY WAS SMALL FOR A FOOTBALL PLAYER, BUT HE DIDN'T LET THAT STOP HIM FROM ACHIEVING HIS DREAM. READ ON TO FIND OUT HOW HE DID IT.

FROM THE TIME HE WAS YOUNG, RUDY LOVED FOOTBA[LL] EVEN THOUGH HE WAS OFTEN THE SMALLEST PLAYER, NO ONE ON THE FIELD TRIED HARDER.

RUDY LOVED NOTRE DAME FOOTBALL MOST OF ALL. EVERYONE IN THE RUETTIGER HOUSEHOLD WAS A FIGHTING IRISH FAN.

> HE'S TO THE **30!** THE **20!**, THE **10!** TOUCHDOWN NOTRE DAME!

> I'M GONNA PLAY FOR THEM ONE DAY.

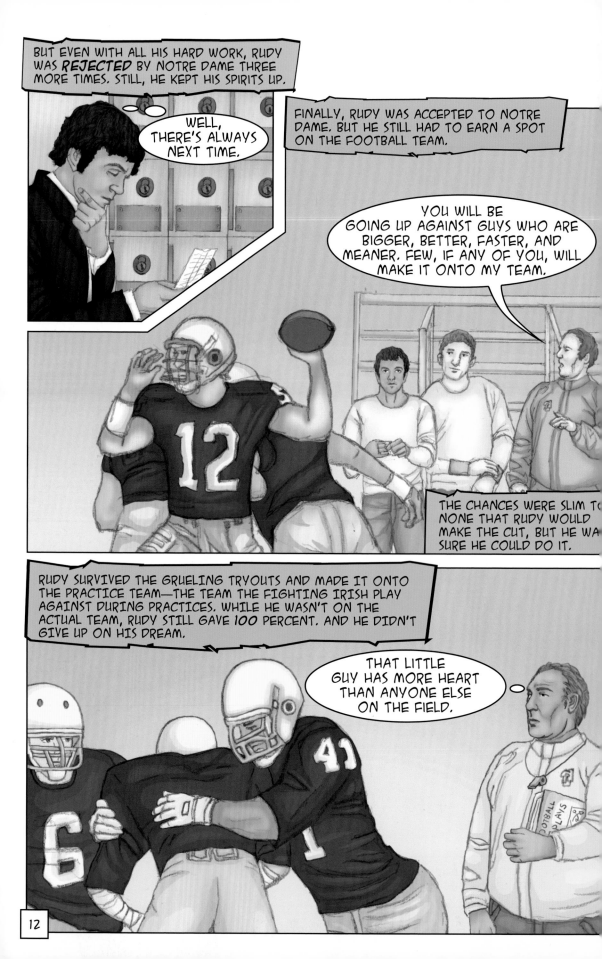

BUT EVEN WITH ALL HIS HARD WORK, RUDY WAS **REJECTED** BY NOTRE DAME THREE MORE TIMES. STILL, HE KEPT HIS SPIRITS UP.

WELL, THERE'S ALWAYS NEXT TIME.

FINALLY, RUDY WAS ACCEPTED TO NOTRE DAME. BUT HE STILL HAD TO EARN A SPOT ON THE FOOTBALL TEAM.

YOU WILL BE GOING UP AGAINST GUYS WHO ARE BIGGER, BETTER, FASTER, AND MEANER. FEW, IF ANY OF YOU, WILL MAKE IT ONTO MY TEAM.

THE CHANCES WERE SLIM TO NONE THAT RUDY WOULD MAKE THE CUT, BUT HE WAS SURE HE COULD DO IT.

RUDY SURVIVED THE GRUELING TRYOUTS AND MADE IT ONTO THE PRACTICE TEAM—THE TEAM THE FIGHTING IRISH PLAY AGAINST DURING PRACTICES. WHILE HE WASN'T ON THE ACTUAL TEAM, RUDY STILL GAVE *100* PERCENT. AND HE DIDN'T GIVE UP ON HIS DREAM.

THAT LITTLE GUY HAS MORE HEART THAN ANYONE ELSE ON THE FIELD.

12

[...DY'S OPTIMISM AND HARD WORK FINALLY [...]ID OFF. THE COACHES HAD HIM DRESS [...]OR A GAME. IN THE FINAL MINUTES, AS [...]E CROWD CHEERED HIS NAME, RUDY [...]OOK THE FIELD.

AS IF THAT WEREN'T ENOUGH, RUDY MADE A TACKLE, HELPING KEEP THE OTHER TEAM FROM SCORING!

RUDY! RUDY!

[...]EAH, RUDY!

ATTA BOY!

[...]DY HAD ACHIEVED HIS DREAM, [...]ANKS TO HIS UNBEATABLE OPTIMISM!

RUDY WAS AN OPTIMIST WHO BELIEVED THAT ANYTHING WAS POSSIBLE. EVEN TODAY, HE LIKES TO GIVE PEOPLE THIS BIT OF ADVICE: "BELIEVE IN YOURSELF AND DON'T LET ANYTHING STOP YOU."

DO YOU BELIEVE IN YOURSELF? HOW HARD WOULD YOU WORK TO ACHIEVE YOUR OWN DREAM?

WHAT WOULD YOU DO?

YOU WANT TO BE AN ARCHITECT SOMEDAY AND DESIGN AMAZING BUILDINGS. YOUR GRADES AREN'T VERY GOOD, THOUGH, AND IT TAKES GOOD GRADES TO GET INTO AN ARCHITECTURE PROGRAM IN COLLEGE. WHAT COULD YOU DO RATHER THAN GIVE UP ON YOUR DREAM?

JEWEL

WHO IS SHE?
MUSICIAN AND ACTRESS

WHY HER?
SHE STAYED OPTIMISTIC THROUGH SOME VERY TRYING TIMES

JEWEL'S LIFE WASN'T EASY—BUT SHE NEVER STOPPED BELIEVING THAT SOMEDAY SHE'D FIND SUCCESS.

JEWEL WAS RAISED OUTSIDE ANCHORAGE, ALASKA. SHE LIVED WITH HER PARENTS AND SEVEN BROTHERS AND SISTERS IN A SMALL LOG CABIN.

HONEY! YOU SHOULD PUT ON YOUR JACKET WHEN YOU GO TO THE OUTHOUSE!

BRRRRR

LIFE WASN'T EASY FOR JEWEL. SHE HAD TO GET UP EARLY AND DO HER CHORES, THEN WALK A LONG DISTANCE TO GET TO SCHOOL.

PLAYING WITH THE QUEEN OF HEARTS, KNOWIN' IT AIN'T REALLY SMART...

BUT JEWEL LOVED WHERE SHE LIVED AND SHE WAS ALWAYS SINGING.

N FACT, MUSIC WAS A BIG PART OF JEWEL'S LIFE. HE AND HER FAMILY WOULD PERFORM FOLK MUSIC AT OTELS, *ESKIMO* VILLAGES, AND TOURIST ATTRACTIONS.

YOU ARE MY SUNSHINE, MY ONLY SUNSHINE...

T THEN THINGS CHANGED. WHEN JEWEL AS EIGHT, HER PARENTS *DIVORCED*.

I'M GOING TO MISS YOU, MAMA.

JEWEL AND HER DAD KEPT PERFORMING— THOUGH SOMETIMES NOT AT THE NICEST PLACES!

WELL, I GUESS THIS IS WHAT THEY CALL GETTING SOME GOOD EXPERIENCE!

T JEWEL HAD BIGGER DREAMS. ONE AS TO GO TO A FAMOUS MUSIC CAMP INTERLOCHEN, MICHIGAN.

HONEY, WE CAN'T AFFORD THAT CAMP.

I KNOW. BUT I THINK I KNOW HOW I CAN RAISE THE MONEY.

JEWEL'S OPTIMISM PAID OFF. SHE DID A SOLO SHOW AT THE LOCAL HIGH SCHOOL AUDITORIUM IN HER HOMETOWN OF HOMER, ALASKA.

WHEN ALL'S SAID AND DONE

I CAN'T BELIEVE HOW THE TOWN HAS SUPPORTED HER. WITH THE MONEY SHE'S RAISED, JEWEL WILL BE ABLE TO GO TO THAT CAMP!

JEWEL STILL HAD SOME TOUGH TIMES AHEAD. ONCE SHE WAS LIVING ON HER OWN, SHE STRUGGLED TO GET BY. SHE TOOK ANY JOB SHE COULD FIND.

WHAT ARE YOU DOING?

I'M TAKING HOME FOOD THE CUSTOMER'S DIDN'T FINISH. IT BEATS STARVING.

TO SAVE MONEY, SHE MOVED INTO HER VAN. SHE PUT ALL OF HER ENERGY INTO WRITING AND PLAYING MUSIC.

WHO WILL SAVE YOUR SOUL... YEAH, THAT SOUNDS GOOD. SOMEDAY PEOPLE ARE GOING TO BE SINGING ALONG WITH THIS SONG!

JEWEL PERFORMED AT SEVERAL LOCAL COFFEEHOUSES. SOON SHE HAD A LOYAL FOLLOWING. IT WASN'T LONG BEFORE RECORD COMPANIES BEGAN TO TAKE NOTICE, TOO!

THESE FOOLISH GAMES...

WOW! WE HAVE TO SIGN THIS GIRL TO OUR RECORD LABEL!

I'VE GOT TO GET THIS GIRL UNDER CONTRACT!

ODAY, JEWEL PLAYS TO SOLD-OUT CROWDS AROUND HE WORLD. SHE HAS SOLD MILLIONS OF ALBUMS, ON AWARDS, AND EVEN APPEARED IN MOVIES.

THANK YOU ALL, THANK YOU ALL VERY MUCH.

JEWEL

YAY JEWEL!

WE LOVE YOU JEWEL!

WOO HOO!

LIFE WASN'T ALWAYS EASY FOR JEWEL. STILL, HER OPTIMISM GOT HER THROUGH THE BAD TIMES AND KEPT HER DREAM ALIVE. COULD YOU STAY AS POSITIVE AS SHE DID?

WHAT WOULD YOU DO?

YOU'VE ALWAYS WANTED TO BE ON T.V. OR IN THE MOVIES. YOU HEAR THAT A PRODUCER IS IN TOWN, GETTING READY TO SHOOT A MOVIE LOCALLY. NEXT WEEKEND, THERE WILL BE OPEN AUDITIONS FOR KIDS YOUR AGE.

"I WANT TO GO," YOU TELL YOUR FAMILY.

"BUT THERE WILL BE THOUSANDS OF KIDS TRYING OUT," THEY SAY. "YOU'LL BE LUCKY TO TALK TO ANYONE."

WHAT WOULD YOU SAY TO YOUR FAMILY? AND WHAT COULD YOU DO TO IMPROVE YOUR CHANCES?

OPTIMISM IN THE FACE OF RACISM

MARTIN LUTHER KING, JR.

WHO IS HE?
U.S. CIVIL RIGHTS LEADER

WHY HIM?
DESPITE COUNTLESS **SETBACKS**, MARTIN REMAINED OPTIMISTIC THAT EQUALITY WOULD BE ACHIEVED

MARTIN FACED SOME DIFFICULT CHALLENGES IN THE FIGHT TO END DISCRIMINATION. STILL, HE NEVER LOST FAITH THAT ONE DAY ALL PEOPLE WOULD BE TREATED EQUALLY. LET'S TAKE A LOOK AT HOW HIS OPTIMISM HELPED AN ENTIRE COUNTRY MOVE TOWARD A BETTER FUTURE.

WHEN MARTIN WAS VERY YOUNG, HE HAD A WHITE FRIEND WHOSE FAMILY OWNED A STORE ACROSS FROM WHERE MARTIN LIVED.

THEY PLAYED TOGETHER EVERY DAY

BUT WHEN THEY WERE OLD ENOUGH TO START KINDERGARTEN, THEY HAD TO GO TO DIFFERENT SCHOOLS. THIS WAS BECAUSE OF **SEGREGATION**-ACTIONS AND LAWS THAT KEPT WHITE AND BLACK PEOPLE APART.

MY DAD SAYS WE CAN'T PLAY TOGETHER ANY MORE.

WHY NOT?

I DON'T KNOW. HE SAYS WE JUST CAN'T. I'M SORRY, MARTIN.

DINNER THAT NIGHT, MARTIN [AS]KED HIS PARENTS WHY HE [SH]OULDN'T PLAY WITH HIS FRIEND.

I KNOW IT DOESN'T MAKE SENSE, SON, BUT THERE ARE A LOT OF WHITE PEOPLE WHO WANT TO KEEP US SEPARATE FROM THEM.

BUT THAT'S NOT FAIR. AND IT MAKES ME MAD.

NOW, HONEY. YOU'VE HEARD THE MESSAGE YOUR FATHER PREACHES AT CHURCH. HE AND I BOTH THINK THAT THE BEST WAY TO FIGHT HATE IS WITH LOVE.

[O]N DECEMBER 1, 1955, A WOMAN NAMED [R]OSA PARKS WAS ARRESTED FOR REFUSING [T]O GIVE UP HER SEAT ON THE BUS TO A [W]HITE MAN.

NO. I WILL NOT MOVE TO THE BACK OF THE BUS.

HER COURAGEOUS ACT MADE PEOPLE THINK [I]T WAS FINALLY TIME FOR A CHANGE. AMONG THOSE PEOPLE WAS MARTIN LUTHER KING, JR.

MARTIN TOOK HIS PARENTS ADVICE TO HEART. WHEN HE GREW UP, HE BECAME A **REVEREND** HIMSELF.

WE MUST DISCOVER THE POWER OF LOVE, THE POWER, THE REDEMPTIVE POWER OF LOVE. *

*ACTUAL QUOTE

IN FACT, HE LED THE PROTEST.

IF THEY WON'T TREAT US FAIRLY ON THEIR BUSES, THEN WE JUST WON'T USE THE BUSES.

BUT HOW ARE WE SUPPOSED TO GET AROUND?

WE'LL WALK. AND THOSE OF US WHO CAN'T WILL TAKE TAXIS. WE SHOULD ARRANGE FOR DRIVERS TO HELP CARPOOL AS WELL.

HIS ROLE IN THE **BOYCOTT** ANGERED MANY PEOPLE. MARTIN WAS FALSELY ARRESTED ON A SPEEDING CHARGE AND TAKEN TO JAIL.

MARTIN'S OPTIMISM WOULD BE TESTED AGAIN DURING A VOTING RIGHTS PROTEST MARCH IN SELMA, ALABAMA.

AS HUNDREDS OF PROTESTERS TRIED TO CROS THE EDMUND PETTIUS BRIDGE ON THEIR WAY TO MONTGOMERY, ALABAMA, THEY WERE ATTACKED BY POLICE AND STATE TROOPERS SENT BY THE GOVERNOR OF ALABAMA.

MARTIN WAS VERY UPSET BY THE ATTACK ON THE PROTESTERS. BUT HE DIDN'T LOSE HOPE—THEY WOULD TRY THE MARCH AGAIN.

I SAY TO YOU I WOULD RATHER DIE ON THE HIGHWAYS OF ALABAMA THAN MAKE A BUTCHERY OF MY CONSCIENCE. *

TWO WEEKS LATER MARTIN LED ANOTHER MARCH. THIS TIME NO POLICE TRIED TO INTERFERE, AND THE PROTESTERS MARCHED ALL THE WAY TO THE STATE CAPITOL BUILDING IN MONTGOMERY.

I MUST ADMIT TO YOU THERE ARE STILL JAIL CELLS WAITING FOR US, DARK AND DIFFICULT MOMENTS. WE WILL GO ON WITH THE FAITH THAT NON-VIOLENCE AND ITS POWER TRANSFORMED DARK YESTERDAY INTO BRIGHT TOMORROWS. WE WILL BE ABLE TO CHANGE THESE CONDITIONS. *

20

* ACTUAL QUOTE

OVER THE YEARS, MARTIN WAS THREATENED, BEATEN, AND ARRESTED, BUT HE NEVER LOST HOPE. HE BELIEVED THAT ONE DAY SEGREGATION IN AMERICA WOULD END.

I SAY TO YOU TODAY, MY FRIENDS, THAT IN SPITE OF THE DIFFICULTIES AND FRUSTRATIONS OF THE MOMENT, I STILL HAVE A DREAM... WITH THIS FAITH WE WILL BE ABLE TO WORK TOGETHER, TO PRAY TOGETHER, TO STRUGGLE TOGETHER, TO GO TO JAIL TOGETHER, TO STAND UP FOR FREEDOM TOGETHER, KNOWING THAT WE WILL BE FREE ONE DAY. *

MARTIN LUTHER KING, JR. WAS ABLE TO STAY OPTIMISTIC IN THE FACE OF HATRED AND INJUSTICE. HIS OPTIMISM MADE A DIFFERENCE. MUCH OF WHAT HE WORKED FOR IS NOW A REALITY.

DO YOU THINK YOU COULD REMAIN OPTIMISTIC IN A SITUATION LIKE THIS? LET'S FIND OUT.

WHAT WOULD YOU DO?

A GROUP OF KIDS FROM ANOTHER SCHOOL ARE CAUSING TROUBLE. THEY SHOW UP IN YOUR NEIGHBORHOOD AND BULLY PEOPLE, OR MAKE FUN OF THEM.

YOUR FRIENDS ARE UPSET AND ANGRY. SOME THINK THERE'S NOTHING ANYONE CAN DO. OTHERS THINK THE ONLY WAY TO CHANGE THINGS IS TO FIGHT BACK. CAN YOU THINK OF A MORE OPTIMISTIC WAY TO DEAL WITH THE SITUATION?

*ACTUAL QUOTE

ELAINE HALL

WHO IS SHE?
FOUNDER OF THE MIRACLE PROJECT

WHY HER?
SHE BELIEVED SHE COULD HELP CHILDREN DO WHAT SOME THOUGHT WAS IMPOSSIBLE.

ELAINE'S OPTIMISM HELPED HER DO SOMETHING AMAZING—STAGE A MUSICAL WRITTEN AND PERFORMED BY CHILDREN WITH *AUTISM*. LET'S SEE HOW SHE DID IT.

ELAINE ADOPTED NEIL FROM RUSSIA WHEN HE WAS VERY LITTLE. AT FIRST, HE SEEMED LIKE ANY OTHER HAPPY, HEALTHY KID.

BUT SOMETHING WAS DIFFERENT ABOUT NEIL. HE OFTEN WOULD GET VERY UPSET. HE ALSO DIDN'T SEEM TO *CONNECT* WITH PEOPLE—NOT EVEN HIS MOTHER.

NEIL? HONEY? COULD YOU LOOK AT ME?

WHEN HE TURNED THREE, NEIL WAS *DIAGNOSED* WITH AUTISM. PEOPLE WITH AUTISM HAVE DIFFICULT *INTERACTING* WITH OTHERS. THEY OFTEN SEEM CLOSED OFF TO THE WORLD AROUND THEM.

BUT ELAINE WAS DETERMINED TO FIND A WAY TO REACH HER SON. AT FIRST, NOTHING SEEMED TO WORK. FINALLY, ELAINE INVITED SOME OF HER FRIENDS OVER TO HELP. THEY WOULD COPY WHAT NEIL WAS DOING AND TURN IT INTO A GAME.

NEIL'S SPINNING. LET'S ALL SPIN!

ELAINE'S OPTIMISM PAID OFF. SLOWLY, NEIL BEGAN TO PLAY WITH HIS MOM AND HER FRIENDS.

LET'S ALL CLAP, JUST LIKE NEIL!

IF THIS IS WORKING FOR NEIL, MAYBE IT WILL HELP OTHER CHILDREN LIKE HIM.

ELAINE FOUNDED THE MIRACLE PROJECT, A MUSICAL THEATER PROGRAM FOR CHILDREN WITH AUTISM. HER PLAN? : TO HELP CHILDREN WITH AUTISM WRITE AND STAR IN THEIR VERY OWN MUSICAL.

THERE ARE ALL THESE MYTHS ABOUT WHAT A CHILD WITH AUTISM CAN DO. I WANT TO SHATTER THEM.

ELAINE SET ABOUT WRITING AND *REHEARSING* THE PLAY—WITH THE HELP OF THE KIDS.

YOU KNOW EVERYTHING THERE IS TO KNOW ABOUT DINOSAURS. DO YOU THINK WE COULD HAVE A DINOSAUR IN OUR PLAY?

A T-REX. WE COULD HAVE A T-REX.

PUTTING ON A PLAY WITH CHILDREN WITH AUTISM WASN'T EASY, BUT ELAINE STAYED OPTIMISTIC WHEN DEALING WITH PROBLEMS.

SUCH AS WHEN KIDS GOT DISCOURAGED...

YOU'RE DOING A GREAT JOB. I'M VERY PROUD OF YOU.

OR THEIR PARENTS BECAME CONCERNED.

I KNOW YOU'RE WORRIED ABOUT KIRA, BUT SHE'S GOING TO BE WONDERFUL, YOU'LL SEE!

...TER MONTHS OF REHEARSING, THE NIGHT ...F THE SHOW ARRIVED. EVERYONE WAS ...ERVOUS, BUT ELAINE STAYED UPBEAT.

ONE PLANET, ONE PEOPLE, ONE SONG.

...HE PLAY WAS A HUGE SUCCESS! ELAINE HAD ...ONE WHAT SEEMED IMPOSSIBLE—AND SHE ...EVER LOST FAITH IN HERSELF OR THE KIDS.

WE DID IT!

WAY TO GO!

GREAT JOB!

ELAINE WANTED TO STAGE A PLAY STARRING KIDS WITH AUTISM—A GOAL MOST PEOPLE WOULD SAY WAS IMPOSSIBLE. BUT SHE NEVER STOPPED BELIEVING THEY COULD DO IT, AND HER OPTIMISM HELPED BOTH HER AND THE KIDS SUCCEED. NOW LET'S SEE WHAT YOU WOULD DO IN A SIMILAR SITUATION.

WHAT WOULD YOU DO?

YOU'VE JUST BEEN TOLD YOUR SCHOOL HAS TO RAISE $20,000 TO KEEP ITS MUSIC PROGRAM GOING. EVERYONE LOVES THE SCHOOL BAND AND MUSIC CLASSES, BUT $20,000 IS A LOT OF MONEY.

"I GUESS THAT'S IT," SAYS ONE OF YOUR FRIENDS. "NO MORE MUSIC FOR US."

WHAT DO YOU THINK? HOW COULD YOU HELP KEEP PEOPLE FEELING OPTIMISTIC AS YOU WORKED TOGETHER TOWARD A SOLUTION?

RED POLLARD AND SEABISCUIT

WHO ARE THEY?
A PROFESSIONAL JOCKEY AND HIS HORSE

WHY THEM?
THEY GAVE HOPE TO A NATION SUFFERING THROUGH THE **GREAT DEPRESSION.**

RED POLLARD AND SEABISCUIT CAME OUT OF NOWHERE TO BECOME CHAMPIONS OF HORSERACING. LET'S SEE HOW THESE TWO UNLIKELY HEROES INSPIRED OPTIMISM IN A COUNTRY THAT DESPERATELY NEEDED IT.

BY 1938, SEABISCUIT AND HIS JOCKEY RED POLLARD WERE CONSIDERED ONE OF THE GREATEST PAIRS IN PROFESSIONAL HORSERACING. THEY WERE CROWD FAVORITES, WINNING RACES, AND SETTING RECORDS AT TRACKS ACROSS THE COUNTRY.

BEFORE THEY MET, HOWEVER, THINGS WEREN'T GOING QUITE SO WELL FOR MAN OR HORSE.

IN 1936, RED POLLARD WAS IN THE FINAL STRETCH OF A LESS-THAN-STELLAR CAREER AS A JOCKEY. HE WAS BLIND IN ONE EYE, HAD NO MONEY, AND SLEPT IN EMPTY HORSE STALLS AT NIGHT.

AS FOR SEABISCUIT, HE WAS SMALLER THAN MOST RACEHORSES, AND WAS KNOWN FOR BEING LAZY AND CRANKY.

C'MON! C'MON! MOVE IT, YOU STUPID HORSE! WE'RE IN LAST PLACE!

BUT RED'S AND SEABISCUIT'S LUCK WAS ABOUT TO CHANGE. RED WAS INTRODUCED TO THE TROUBLESOME HORSE BY ITS TRAINER, TOM SMITH. THE TWO HIT IT OFF RIGHT AWAY.

HERE YOU GO, BOY. MY NAME'S RED.

I THINK SEABISCUIT JUST PICKED HIS NEW JOCKEY.

RED KNEW JUST HOW TO HANDLE THE HORSE. IT WASN'T LONG BEFORE HE AND SEABISCUIT STARTED RACING TOGETHER AND WINNING! THE PAIR TOOK THE RACING WORLD BY STORM.

COME ON, BOY! LET'S SHOW 'EM WHAT YOU CAN DO!

AT THAT SAME TIME, AMERICA WAS GOING THROUGH THE GREAT DEPRESSION. PEOPLE WERE OUT OF WORK, HUNGRY, AND LOSING THEIR HOMES.

PEOPLE DESPERATELY NEEDED SOMETHING TO LIFT THEIR SPIRITS AND HELP THEM BELIEVE THEY WOULD MAKE IT THROUGH THIS DIFFICULT TIME.

FOR ALL THOSE PEOPLE, RED AND SEABISCUIT BECAME *SYMBOLS* OF HOPE AND OPTIMISM. THEY WERE UNDERDOGS, LOSERS WHO HAD TURNED THEIR LUCK AROUND TO BECOME WINNERS.

...EIR LEGEND ONLY GREW AS BOTH HORSE ...D RIDER ENCOUNTERED SETBACKS. FIRST, ...D'S LEG WAS CRUSHED IN AN ACCIDENT. ...ANY WERE AFRAID HE WOULD NEVER ...PE AGAIN.

BUT EVEN WITH A NEW JOCKEY, SEABISCUIT TRIUMPHED OVER TRIPLE CROWN WINNER WAR ADMIRAL IN WHAT WAS BILLED THE "MATCH OF THE CENTURY."

HE WINS! SEABISCUIT WINS!

...O YEARS LATER, RED POLLARD ...S BACK IN THE SADDLE, RIDING ...ABISCUIT TO EVEN MORE ...CTORIES. NEITHER THE HORSE ...OR HIS RIDER EVER STOPPED ...LIEVING THEY WERE WINNERS.

WHETHER THEY KNEW IT OR NOT, RED POLLARD AND SEABISCUIT WEREN'T JUST RACING FOR THEMSELVES. THEY WERE RACING FOR EVERY AMERICAN LOOKING TO ESCAPE THE GRIM DAY-TO-DAY MISERY OF THE GREAT DEPRESSION.

PEOPLE BELIEVED THAT IF RED AND SEABISCUIT COULD KEEP WINNING AGAINST OVERWHELMING ODDS, THEN MAYBE THEY COULD TOO. COULD YOU INSPIRE THE SAME KIND OF OPTIMISM?

WHAT WOULD YOU DO?

A FRIEND OF YOURS IS GOING THROUGH A TOUGH TIME. HIS DAD IS SICK, AND HIS FAMILY IS HAVING TROUBLE PAYING BILLS. WHAT COULD YOU SAY OR DO TO MAKE HIM FEEL OPTIMISTIC ABOUT THE FUTURE?

WEB SITES

TO LEARN MORE ABOUT PARKINSON'S DISEASE, VISIT THIS SITE.

www.parkinsons.org

FIND OUT EVERYTHING THERE IS TO KNOW ABOUT AUTISM, AND WHAT YOU CAN DO TO HELP.

www.autism-society.org

FIND OUT MORE ABOUT ELAINE HALL AND THE MIRACLE PROJECT.

www.themiracleproject.org

TO LEARN MORE ABOUT MARTIN LUTHER KING, JR. AND HIS LEGACY, VISIT THE KING CENTER.

www.thekingcenter.org

READ ABOUT THE LIFE AND TIMES OF RED POLLARD AND HIS HORSE SEABISCUIT.

www.pbs.org/wgbh/amex/seabiscuit/mammalsevents/
m_pollard.html

LEARN MORE ABOUT JEWEL, HER MUSIC, AND HER LIFE.

www.atlanticrecords.com/jewel

FIND OUT MORE ABOUT DANIEL RUETTIGER AND HIS INSPIRATIONAL STORY.

www.rudyinternational.com

GLOSSARY

AUTISM A DEVELOPMENT DISORDER THAT AFFECTS THE BRAIN AND CAN MAKE COMMUNICATING AND INTERACTING WITH OTHERS DIFFICULT

BOYCOTT REFUSING TO BUY OR USE SOMETHING

CIVIL RIGHTS RIGHTS THAT GUARANTEE ALL CITIZENS EQUAL OPPORTUNITIES

CONNECT TO HAVE A RELATIONSHIP

DIAGNOSE TO FIND OUT WHAT IS WRONG

DIVORCE THE END OF A MARRIAGE

ESKIMO NATIVE PEOPLE OF NORTHERN CANADA, ALASKA, GREENLAND, AND EASTERN SIBERIA

GREAT DEPRESSION A SERIOUS FINANCIAL SLUMP THAT BEGAN IN 1929

INTERACT TO TALK, SING, DANCE, ARGUE, AND LAUGH, WITH OTHER PEOPLE

PARKINSON'S DISEASE A DISEASE OF THE BRAIN (CENTRAL NERVOUS SYSTEM) THAT AFFECTS MOTOR SKILLS, SPEECH, AND OTHER FUNCTIONS

POPULARITY BEING LIKED BY OTHERS

REHEARSING PRACTICING FOR A PERFORMANCE

REJECTED TO BE REFUSED BY SOMEONE OR SOMETHING

REVEREND A TITLE USED TO ADDRESS MEMBERS OF THE CLERGY

SEGREGATION KEEPING PEOPLE OF DIFFERENT RACES APART

SETBACK A REVERSAL IN PROCESS; A BARRIER TO ACHIEVING GOALS

SYMBOL SOMETHING THAT STANDS FOR SOMETHING ELSE

TREATMENT MEDICAL CARE

TRANSFER TO MOVE

INDEX